FOR THE YOUNG BEGINNER

Notespeller Book

Level E

Students who read fluently will be able to enjoy playing the piano for a lifetime. The activities in this NOTESPELLER BOOK aid students in developing reading skills and recognizing interval and chord patterns. Concepts are reinforced through games, puzzles, coloring pages and written exercises. Students are encouraged to play many of the notated examples to further enhance the reading process. This book provides an enjoyable and appealing way to have fun while learning valuable musical skills!

Instructions for Use

1. This NOTESPELLER is designed to be used with Alfred's PREP COURSE for the young beginner, LESSON BOOK E. It can also serve as an effective supplement for other piano methods.

2. This book is coordinated page-by-page with the LESSON BOOK, and assignments are ideally made according to the instructions in the upper right corner of each page of the NOTESPELLER.

3. This NOTESPELLER reinforces note reading concepts presented in the LESSON BOOK through coloring and written exercises.

Gayle Kowalchyk • E. L. Lancaster

Copyright © MCMXCV by Alfred Music
All rights reserved. Produced in USA.
ISBN-10: 0-7390-2500-7
ISBN-13: 978-0-7390-2500-0
Cover illustration and interior art by Christine Finn

*Use with Alfred's Basic Piano Library,
PREP COURSE, Lesson Book E, page 4.*

Connect-the-Dots Puzzle
(Harmonic Interval Review)

1. Draw lines connecting the dots on the matching boxes.

2. Write the interval name (2, 3, 4 or 5) on the line.

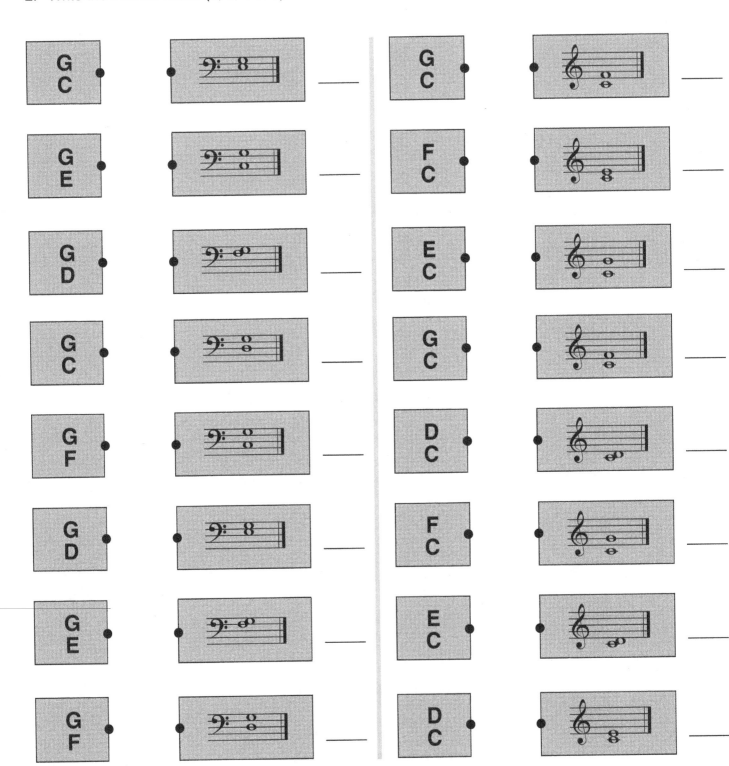

Naming Line Notes on the Grand Staff

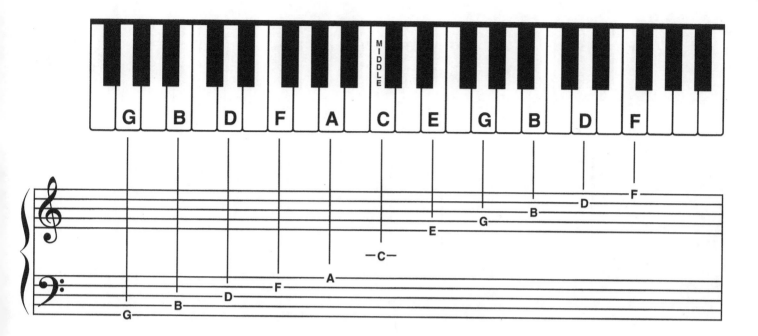

1. Write the names of the line notes on the grand staff. Begin with the bass staff.

2. Write the name of each note in the square below it.

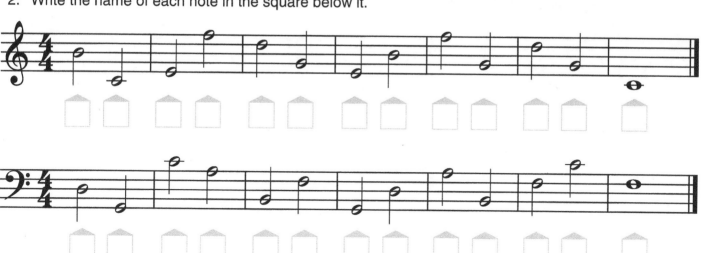

4

Use with page 8.

Naming Space Notes on the Grand Staff

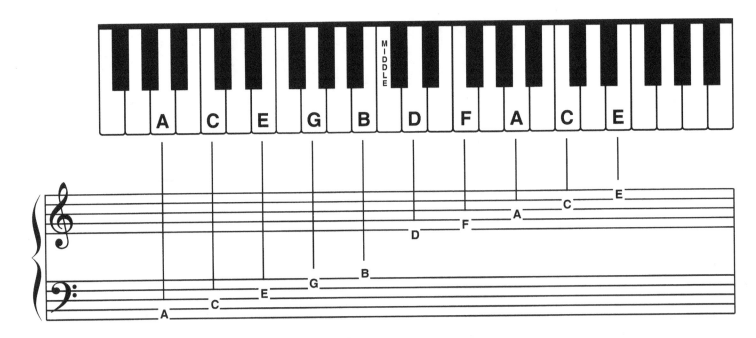

1. Write the names of the space notes on the grand staff. Begin with the bass staff.

2. Write the name of each note in the square below it.

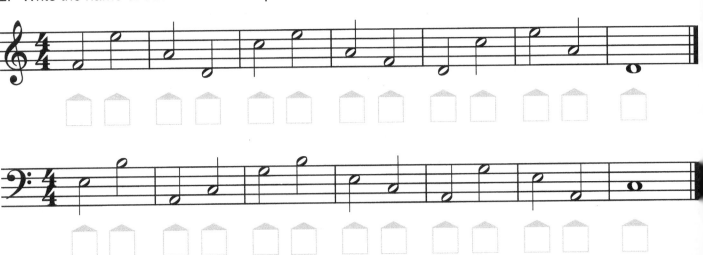

Coloring Harmonic Intervals

Connect-the-Dots Puzzle

Draw lines connecting the dots on the matching boxes.

Use with page 10.

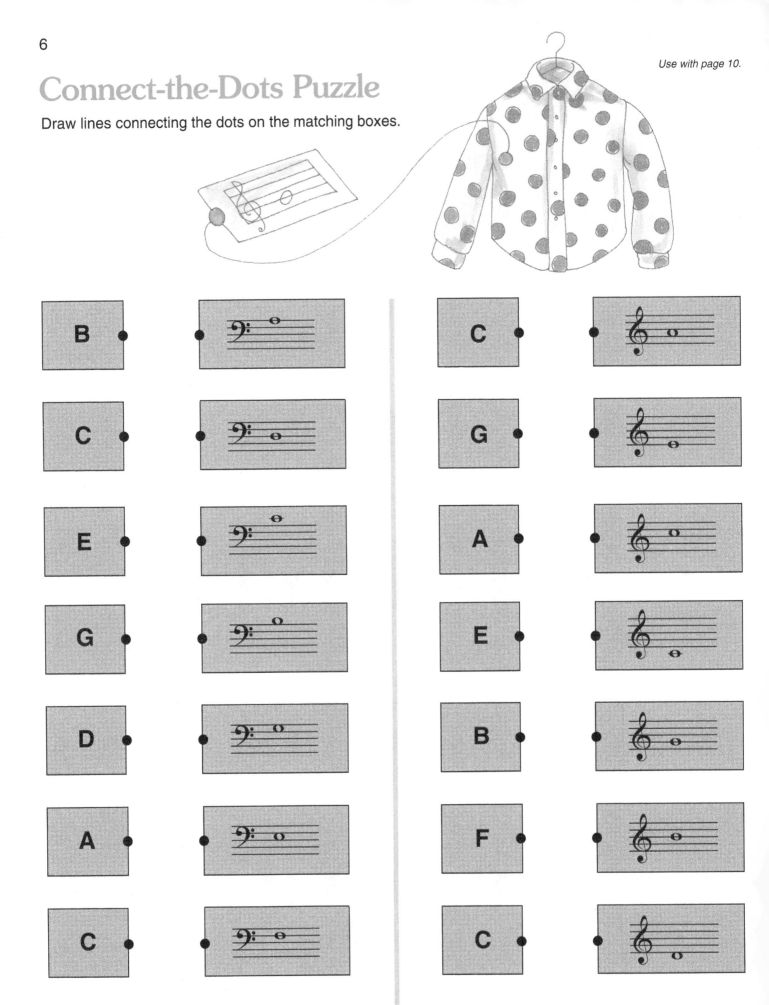

Note Match-Up

Circle the notes that match each group of letters.

1. D D E C

2. G E C E

3. F G E

4. E F D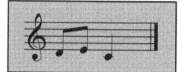

5. G F E G

6. E D C E

7. D E F

8. F E D F

Use with page 12.

Measuring 6ths

When you skip 4 white keys, the interval is a **6th.**

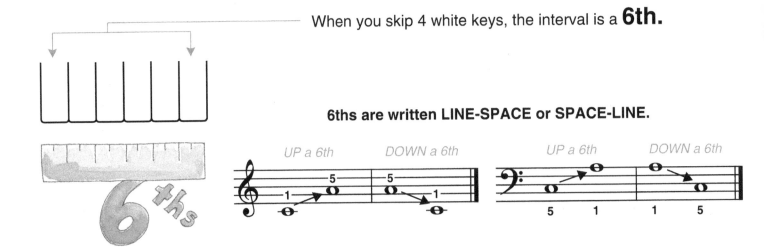

6ths are written LINE-SPACE or SPACE-LINE.

1. Draw a half note UP a 6th from each C and DOWN a 6th from each A on the staffs below.

2. Write the name of each note in the square below it—then play and say the note name.

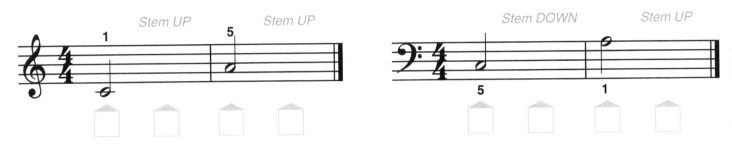

3. Draw a whole note ABOVE the given note in each measure below
   to make the indicated harmonic interval.

4. Write the names of the notes in the squares. Write the name of the lower note
   in the lower square; the name of the higher note in the higher square.

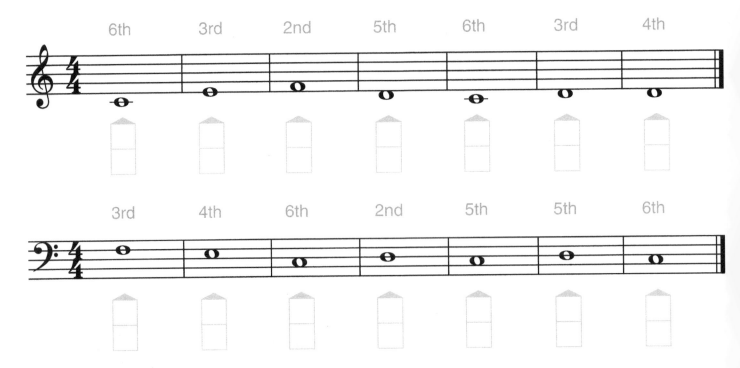

Drawing Intervals

1. Draw a half note DOWN from the given note in each measure below to make the indicated melodic interval. Turn all the stems UP.

2. Write the name of each note in the square below it.

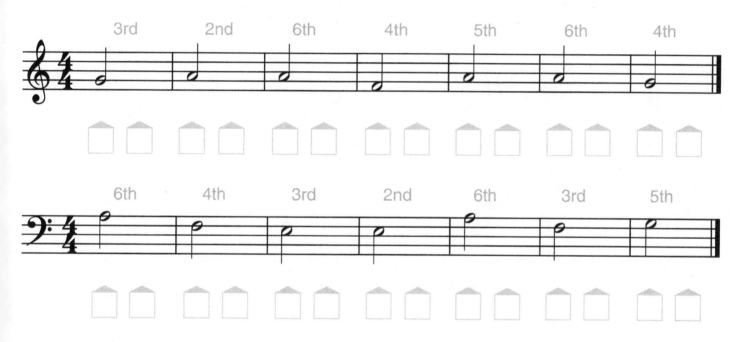

3. Draw a whole note BELOW the given note to make the indicated harmonic interval.

4. Write the names of the notes in the squares. Write the name of the lower note in the lower square; the name of the higher note in the higher square.

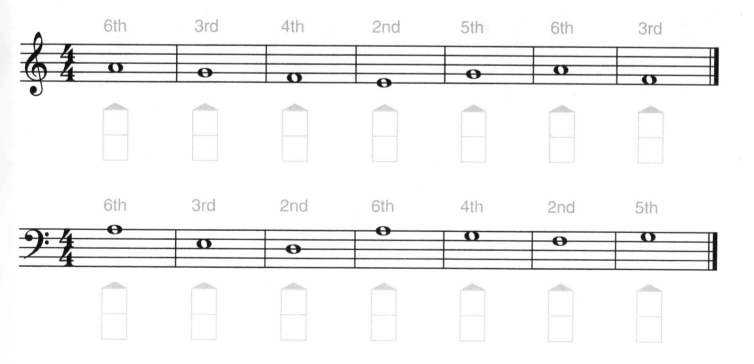

Connect-the-Dots Puzzle

(Interval Review)

Use with page 14.

1. Draw lines connecting the dots on the matching boxes.

2. Write the interval name (2, 3, 4, 5 or 6) on the line.

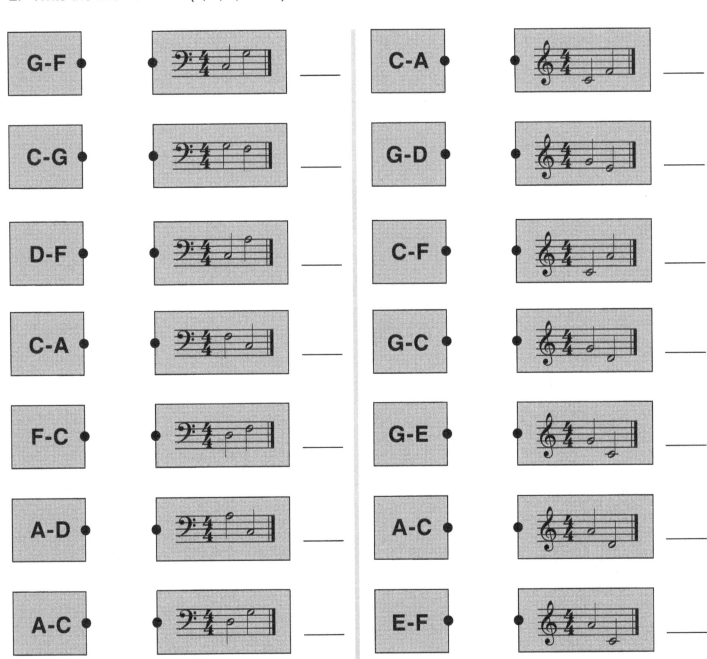

Crossword Puzzle
Note Review

Solve the crossword puzzle
by writing the names of the
notes in the squares.

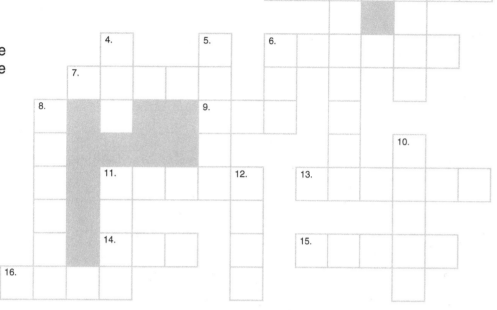

Across

Down

Use with page 16.

Interval and Key Matching Game

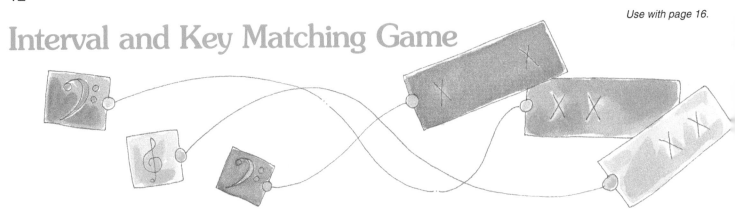

1. Draw lines connecting the dots to match the intervals to their locations on the keyboard.

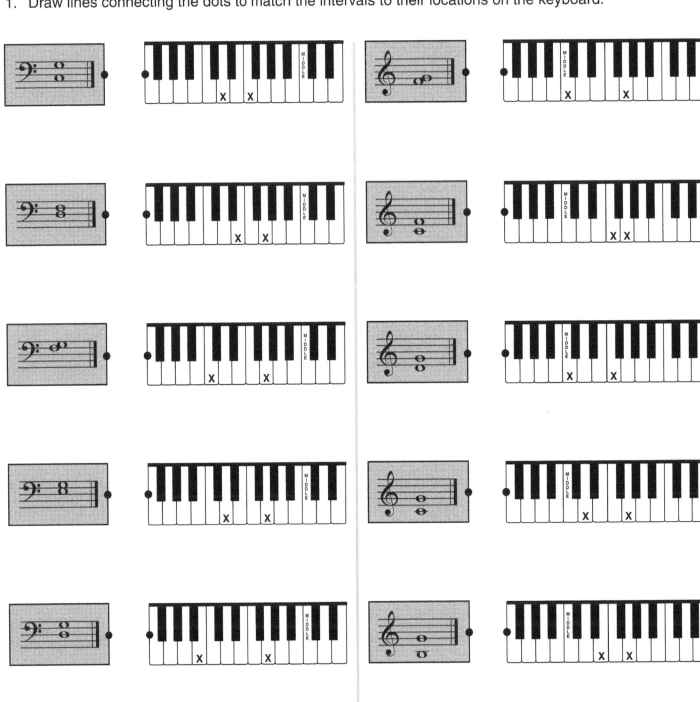

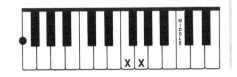

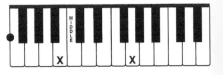

Coloring Harmonic Intervals

1. Color the keys on the keyboard ORANGE for the 2nds.
2. Color the keys on the keyboard RED for the 3rds.
3. Color the keys on the keyboard BLUE for the 4ths.
4. Color the keys on the keyboard GREEN for the 5ths.
5. Color the keys on the keyboard PURPLE for the 6ths.

a.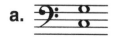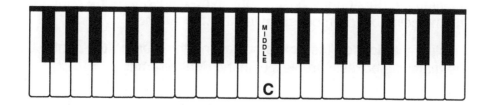

b.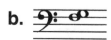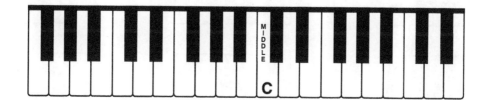

c.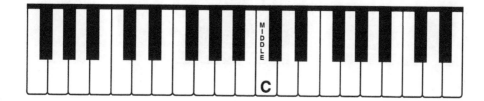

d.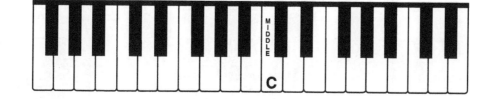

e.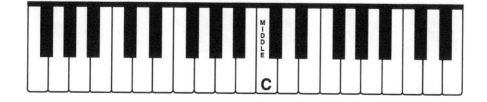

f.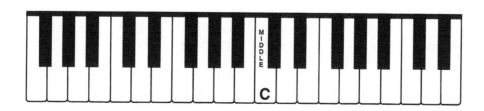

Use with pages 18–19.

Word Match-Up
(Note Review)

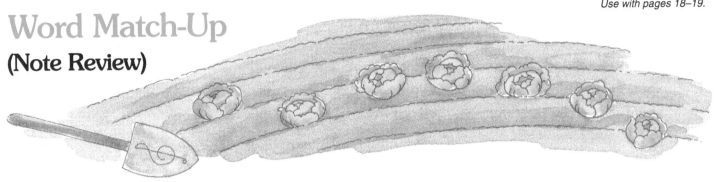

1. Draw lines connecting the dots on the boxes containing the word in the center column to the dots on the matching boxes in bass clef in the left column.

2. Draw lines connecting the dots on the boxes containing the word in the center column to the dots on the matching boxes in treble clef in the right column.

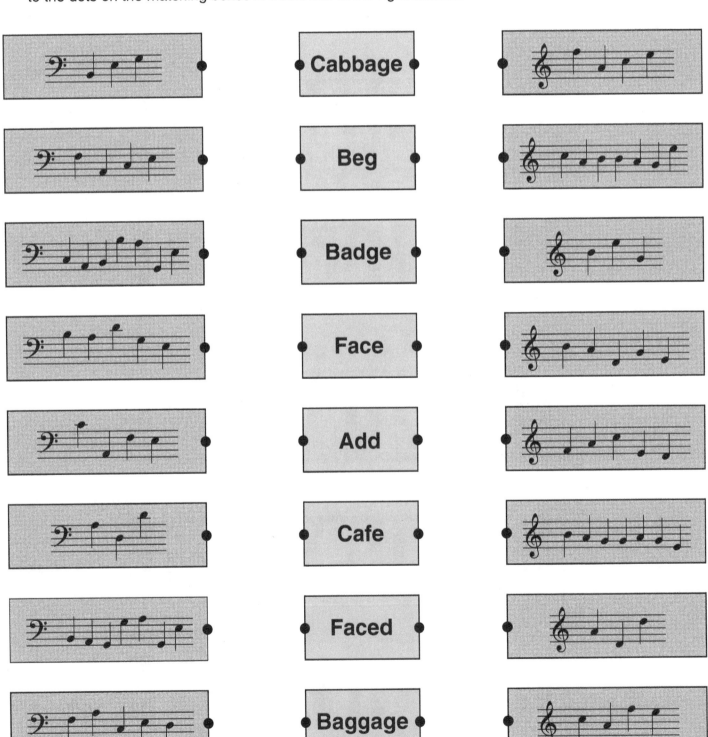

Cabbage

Beg

Badge

Face

Add

Cafe

Faced

Baggage

Connect-the-Dots Puzzle
(Interval Review)

Use with pages 20–21.

1. Draw lines connecting the dots on the matching boxes.

2. Write the interval name (2, 3, 4, 5 or 6) on the line.

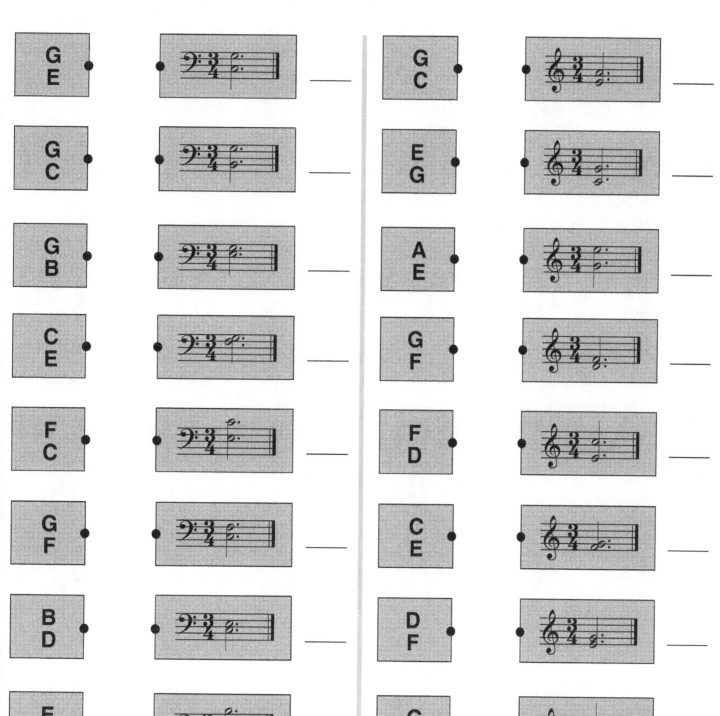

Use with page 22.

Interval and Key Matching Game

1. Draw lines connecting the dots to match the 6ths to their locations on the keyboard.

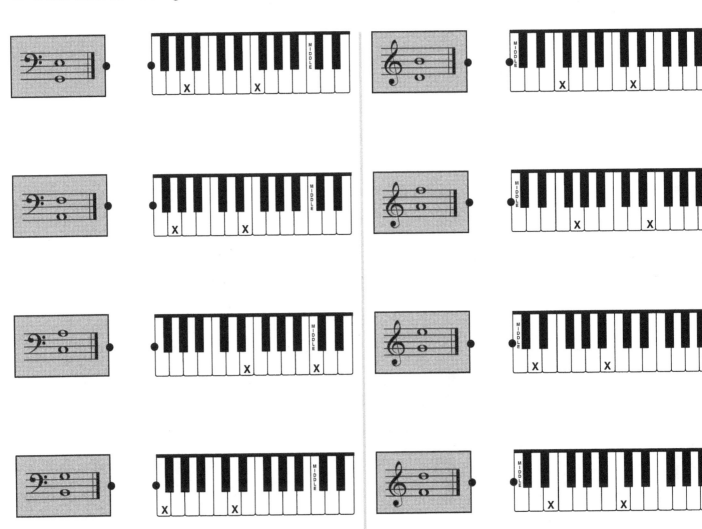

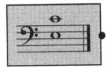 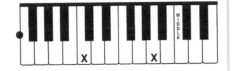  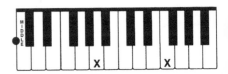

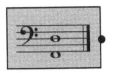 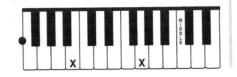  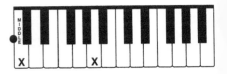

Coloring 6ths

1. Color the keys on the keyboard RED for the melodic 6ths.

2. Color the keys on the keyboard GREEN for the harmonic 6ths.

a.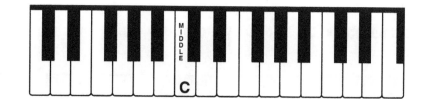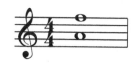

b.

c.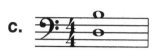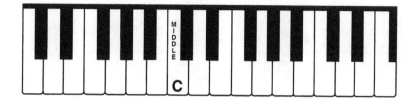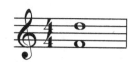

d.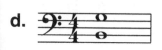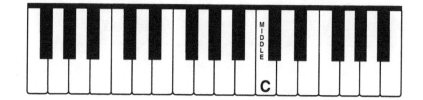

e.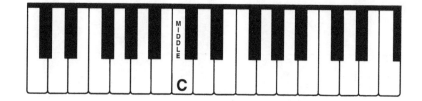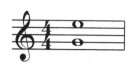

f.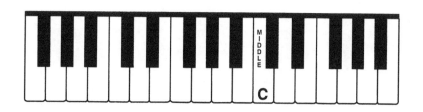

Broken Chord Match-Up

Use with pages 26–27.

Circle the broken chord pattern on the staff that matches the letter names.

1. E G♯ B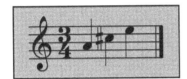

2. F A C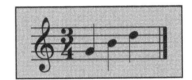

3. G B D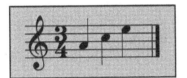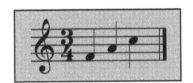

4. A C E

5. G B D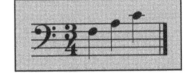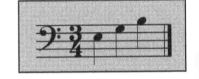

6. F A C

7. E G B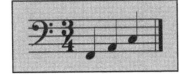

Measuring 7ths

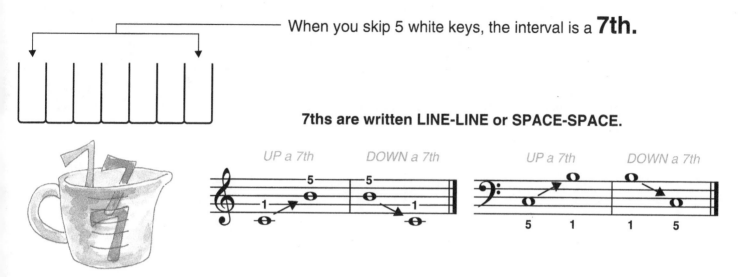

When you skip 5 white keys, the interval is a **7th.**

7ths are written LINE-LINE or SPACE-SPACE.

UP a 7th   DOWN a 7th   UP a 7th   DOWN a 7th

1. Draw a half note UP a 7th from each C, and DOWN a 7th from each B on the staffs below.

2. Write the name of each note in the square below it—then play and say the note name.

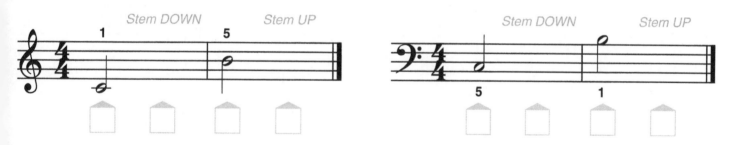

Stem DOWN   Stem UP   Stem DOWN   Stem UP

3. Draw a whole note ABOVE the given note in each measure below to make the indicated harmonic interval.

4. Write the names of the notes in the squares. Write the name of the lower note in the lower square; the name of the higher note in the higher square.

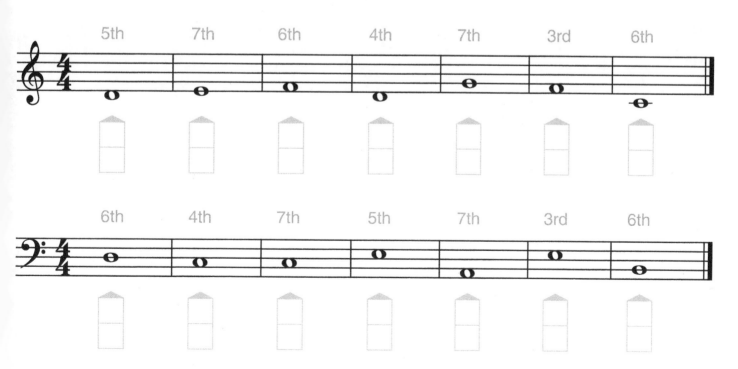

20

Drawing Intervals

Use with page 29.

1. Draw a half note DOWN from the given note in each measure below to make the indicated melodic interval. Turn all the stems UP.

2. Write the name of each note in the square below it.

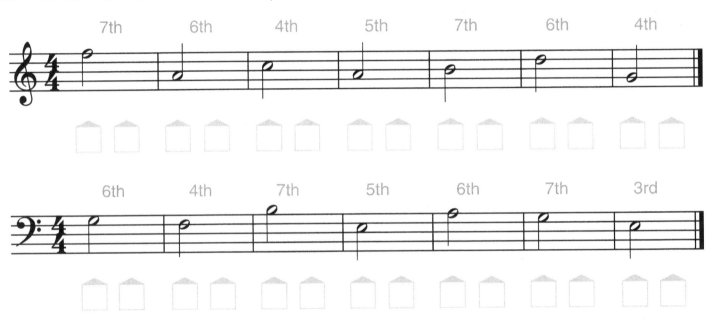

3. Draw a whole note BELOW the given note to make the indicated harmonic interval.

4. Write the names of the notes in the squares. Write the name of the lower note in the lower square; the name of the higher note in the higher square.

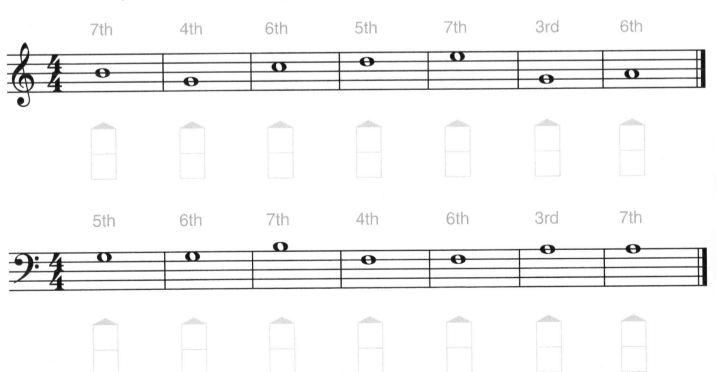

Connect-the-Dots
(Interval Review)

1. Draw lines connecting the dots on the matching boxes.

2. Write the interval name (2, 3, 4, 5, 6 or 7) on the line.

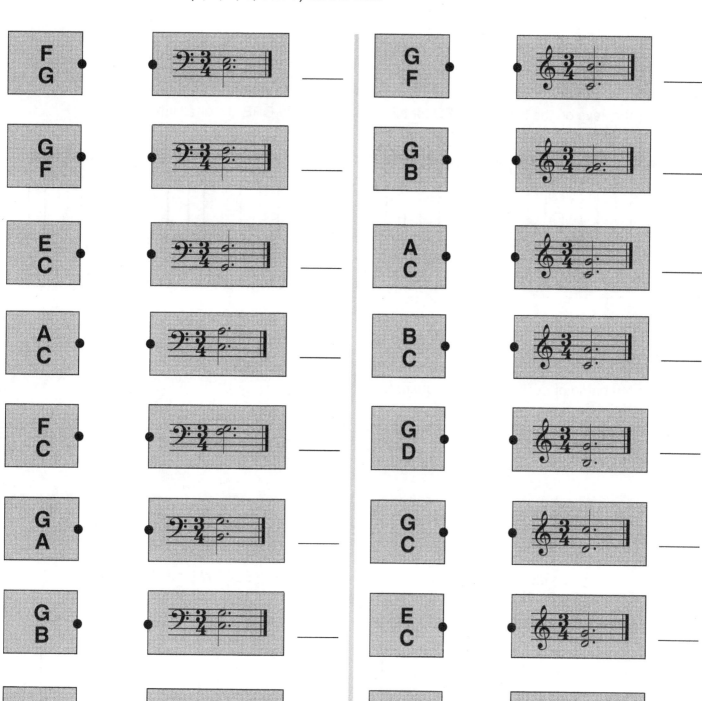

Use with page 32.

Writing Missing Notes and Coloring Scales

1. Write the missing notes from the C MAJOR SCALE on the TREBLE staff below. Use WHOLE NOTES.

2. Write the name of each note in the square below it.

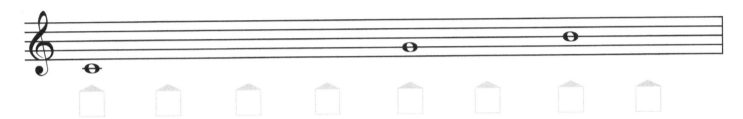

3. Color the keys on the keyboard RED for all space notes and GREEN for all line notes in the C MAJOR SCALE written on the treble staff above.

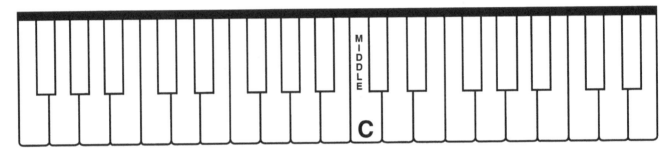

4. Write the missing notes from the C MAJOR SCALE on the BASS staff below. Use WHOLE NOTES.

5. Write the name of each note in the square below it.

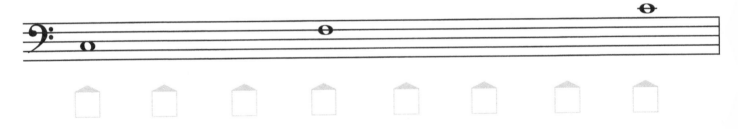

6. Color the keys on the keyboard BLUE for all space notes and YELLOW for all line notes in the C MAJOR SCALE written on the bass staff above.

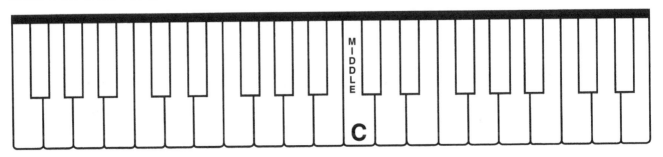

Writing the C Major Scale

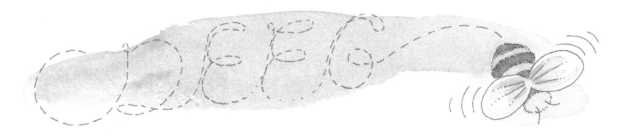

1. Write the notes of the C MAJOR SCALE in the TREBLE staff under the squares.
   Use WHOLE NOTES.

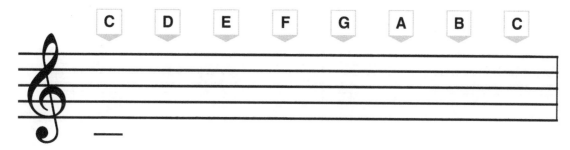

2. Write the notes of the C MAJOR SCALE in the BASS staff over the squares.
   Use WHOLE NOTES.

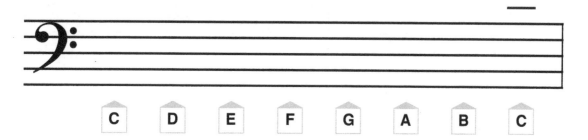

3. Write the name of each note in the square below it—then play and say the note names.

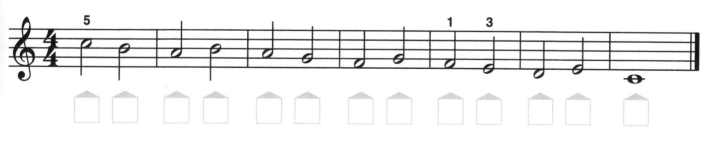

Use with pages 34–35.

Name the Notes
(Harmonic Intervals)

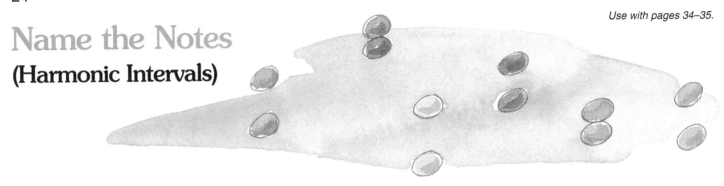

1. Draw a whole note BELOW the given note to make the indicated harmonic interval.

2. Write the names of the notes in the squares. Write the name of the lower note in the lower square, the name of the higher note in the higher square.

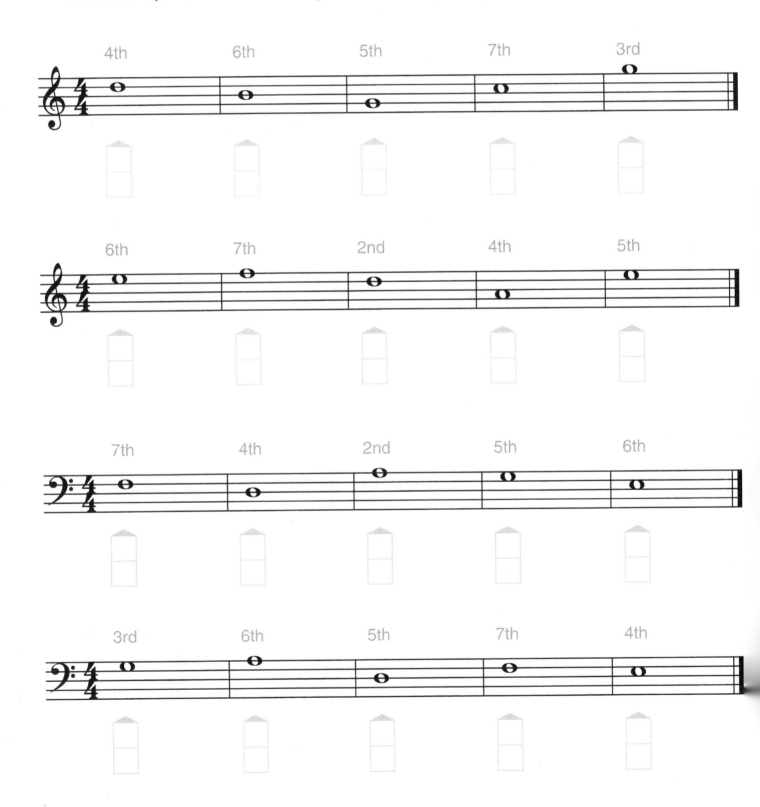

Measuring Octaves (8ths)

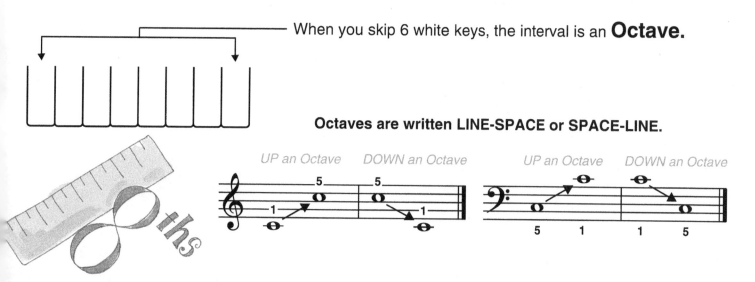

When you skip 6 white keys, the interval is an **Octave.**

Octaves are written LINE-SPACE or SPACE-LINE.

1. Draw a half note UP an octave from the lower C and DOWN an octave from the higher C on the staffs below.

2. Write the name of each note in the square below it—then play and say the note name.

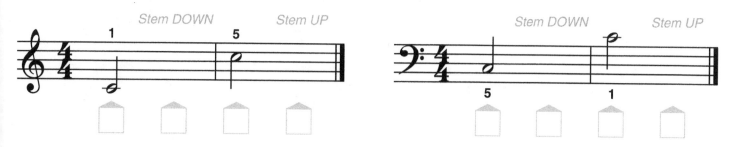

3. Draw a whole note ABOVE the given note in each measure below to make the indicated harmonic interval.

4. Write the names of the notes in the squares. Write the name of the lower note in the lower square; the name of the higher note in the higher square.

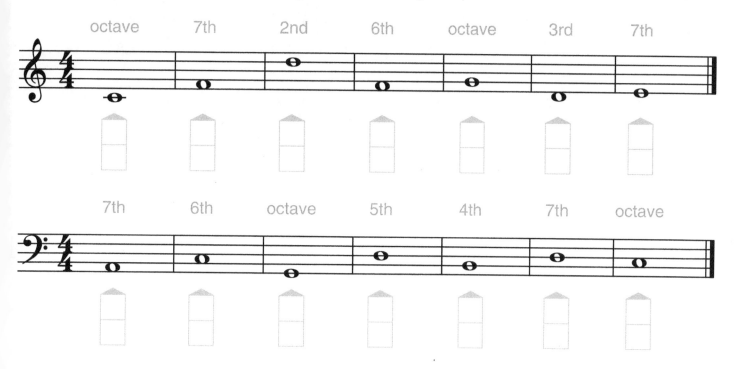

Use with page 37.

Connect-the-Dots Puzzle

(Interval Review)

1. Draw lines connecting the dots on the matching boxes.

2. Write the interval name (4, 5, 6, 7 or 8) on the line.

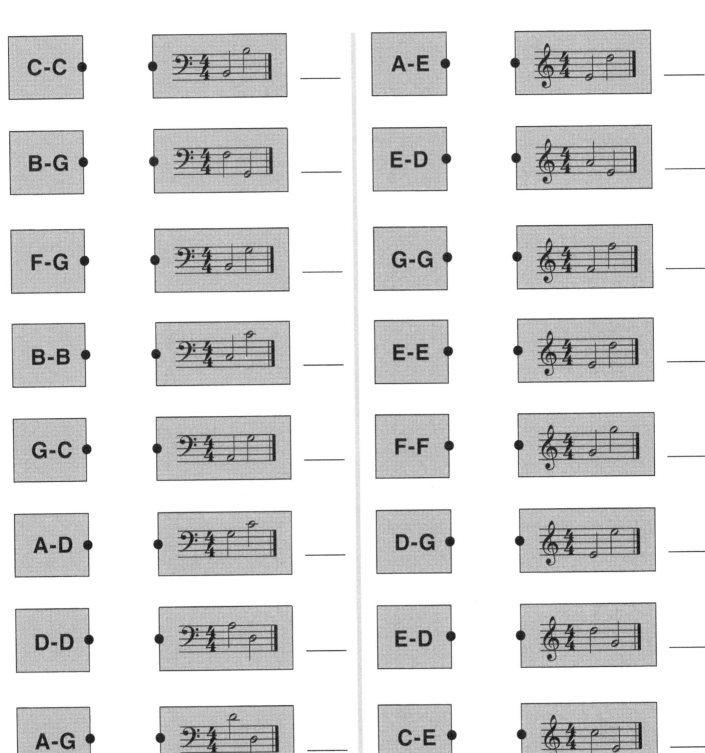

Name the Notes

Use with pages 38–39.

Write the name of each note in the square below it—
then play and say the note names.

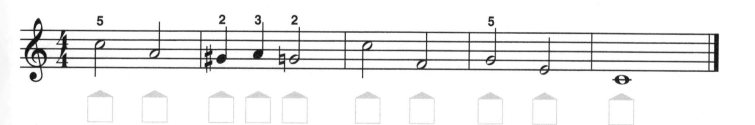

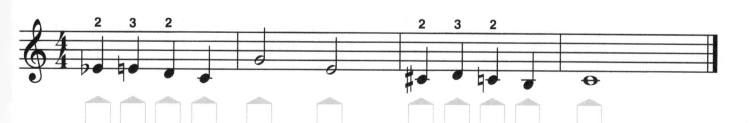

Writing Missing Notes and Coloring Scales

Use with page 40.

1. Write the missing notes from the G MAJOR SCALE on the TREBLE staff below. Use WHOLE NOTES.

2. Write the name of each note in the square below it.

3. Color the keys on the keyboard RED for all space notes and GREEN for all line notes in the G MAJOR SCALE written on the treble staff above.

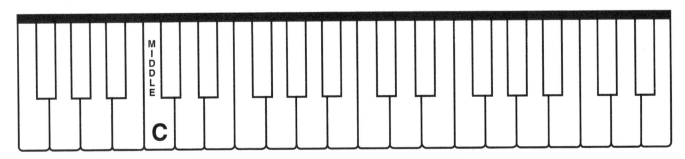

4. Write the missing notes from the G MAJOR SCALE on the BASS staff below. Use WHOLE NOTES.

5. Write the name of each note in the square below it.

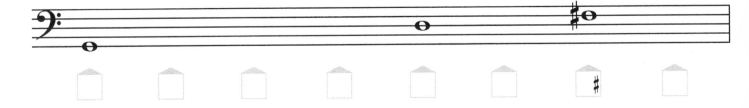

6. Color the keys on the keyboard BLUE for all space notes and YELLOW for all line notes in the G MAJOR SCALE written on the bass staff above.

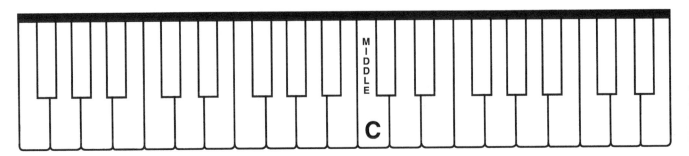

Writing the G Major Scale

1. Write the notes of the G MAJOR SCALE in the TREBLE staff under the squares.
   Use WHOLE NOTES.

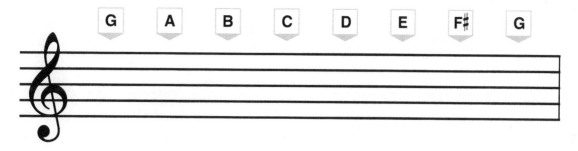

| G | A | B | C | D | E | F# | G |

2. Write the notes of the G MAJOR SCALE in the BASS staff over the squares.
   Use WHOLE NOTES.

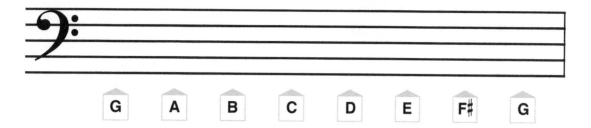

| G | A | B | C | D | E | F# | G |

3. Write the name of each note in the square below it—
   then play and say the note names.

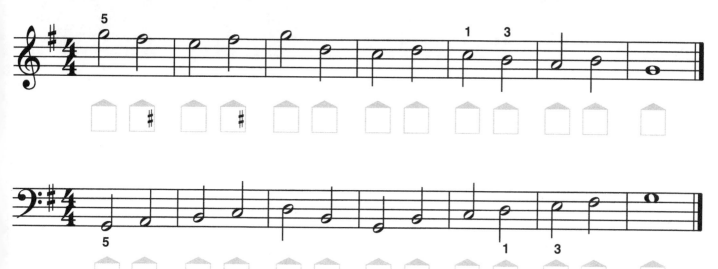

Note Match-Up

Use with pages 42–43.

Circle the notes that match each group of letters.

1. **GFEE**

2. **CCBA**

3. **FFED**

4. **DBGG**

5. **CGEG**

6. **BGFG**

7. **GDBD**

8. **ADCD**

Word Match-Up
(Note Review)

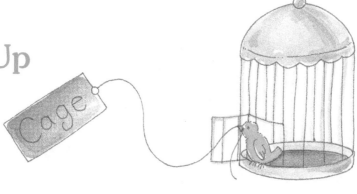

1. Draw lines connecting the dots on the boxes containing the word in the center column to the dots on the matching boxes in bass clef in the left column.

2. Draw lines connecting the dots on the boxes containing the word in the center column to the dots on the matching boxes in treble clef in the right column.

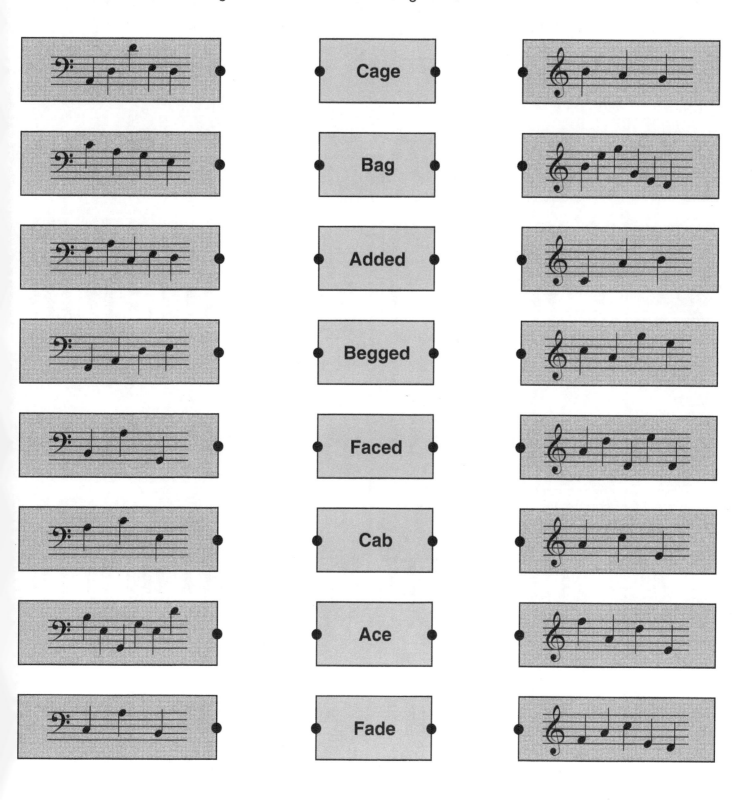

Interval and Key Matching Game

Use with pages 46–47.

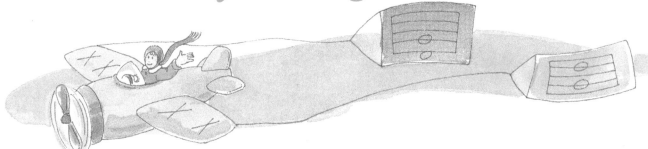

1. Draw lines connecting the dots to match the intervals to their locations on the keyboard.

 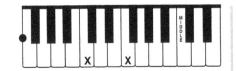  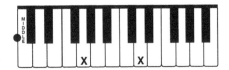

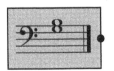 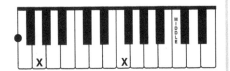  

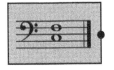 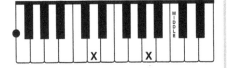  

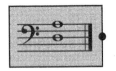 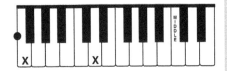  

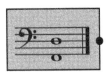 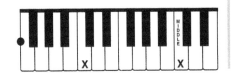  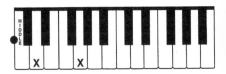